EVERYTHING YOU KNOW ABOUT BIRDS IS WRONG!

DR NICK CRUMPTON
and GAVIN SCOTT

TO JESS, WHO TAUGHT ME ALMOST
EVERYTHING IN THIS BOOK.

N. C.

FOR NOAH, ELIJAH AND FRASER.

G. S.

First published 2026 by Nosy Crow Ltd
Wheat Wharf, 27a Shad Thames,
London, SE1 2XZ, UK

Nosy Crow Eireann Ltd
44 Orchard Grove, Kenmare,
Co Kerry, V93 FY22, Ireland
www.nosycrow.com

ISBN 978 1 83994 946 3

Nosy Crow and associated logos are trademarks
and/or registered trademarks of Nosy Crow Ltd.

Text © Nick Crumpton 2026
Illustrations © Gavin Scott 2026

With very special thanks to Dr Alex Bond for his contributions and advice.

The right of Nick Crumpton to be identified as the author and Gavin Scott
to be identified as the illustrator of this work has been asserted.

All rights reserved.

This book is sold subject to the condition that it shall not, by way of trade or otherwise,
be lent, hired out or otherwise circulated in any form of binding or cover other than that in
which it is published. No part of this publication may be reproduced, stored in a retrieval system,
or transmitted in any form or by any means (electronic, mechanical, photocopying, recording
or otherwise) without the prior written permission of Nosy Crow Ltd.

The publisher and copyright holders prohibit the use of either text or illustrations to develop any
generative machine learning artificial intelligence (AI) models or related technologies.

A CIP catalogue record for this book is available from the British Library.

Printed in China following rigorous ethical sourcing standards.

1 3 5 7 9 8 6 4 2

CONTENTS

Introduction	4–5
We know what the first bird looked like	6–7
Velociraptor was the last raptor	8–9
Birds that look alike are always related	10–11
Birds' super-sight is their strongest sense	12–13
Flying is easy	14–15
Birds are unclean	16–17
Birds are defenceless	18–19
All birds eat seeds	20–21
Owls only come out at night	22–23
Birdsong sounds lovely	24–25
Birds can speak	26–27
People think all birds are beautiful	28–29
It's easy for birds to find a partner	30–31
Dodos were silly	32–33
Seagulls are mean	34–35
Birdwatchers just watch birds	36–37
Birdwatching isn't for everyone	38–39
Penguins only live at the South Pole	40–41
Nests are round and made of twigs	42–43
Birds aren't very smart	44–45
Pigeons are pests	46–47
Birds and people don't mix	48–49
All birds make great pets	50–51
Baby birds are adorable	52–53
Birds aren't at risk	54–55
We can't help birds	56–57
We have discovered all the birds	58–59
Now we know it all	60–61
Glossary	62–63
Index	64

INTRODUCTION

If you take a walk outside, the first animal you'll see will *probably* be a BIRD. Insects will be crawling everywhere, there'll most likely be some sort of fluffy mammal asleep in a nearby tree and it's fish-town if you're near the sea! But even though life is all around you, you'll almost certainly spot a bird first: perching on a tree branch, skittering along a garden fence or soaring across the sky above your head. Feathery, flappy birds: they're everywhere!

The problem with things you see everywhere is that the more you see them, the less you notice them! After a while, birds become part of the scenery. They sort of blend into the background and become . . . BORING!

Well, that – along with a lot of things you've probably been told about birds – is just plain untrue.

Life on Earth is ALWAYS surprising when you really look at it. And birds are especially astonishing. Sure, a shark might be a fearsome predator, but did you know there are birds that eat other animals' bones? And, yeah, cheetahs are record-breaking runners, but the fastest animal on Earth is covered in feathers, not fur!

In fact, there are over 11,000 species of birds flying, paddling and scampering around on our little planet, and that incredible diversity means that there are birds of almost every colour, size and personality. There are birds that use tools, birds that build towers and even birds that work with humans. They migrate further than any other animal on the planet, can see more colours than we could imagine and some are even able to sense Earth's invisible magnetic field.

So, forget about mean seagulls, bread-scoffing ducks and dirty pigeons. This book is going to show you that birds are brilliant and breathtaking, and that everything you think you know about them . . . is WRONG!

WE KNOW WHAT THE FIRST BIRD LOOKED LIKE

WRONG!

You can't start a book about birds without talking about dinosaurs – the reptiles that ruled the roost (Earth, that is) for a gargantuan 170 MILLION years. You might have heard that the first bird to evolve from their dinosaur ancestors was the tooth-beaked, long-tailed *ARCHAEOPTERYX*.
Well . . . that's just WRONG!

JURASSIC PERIOD
(200–145 MILLION YEARS AGO)

One of the things that all true birds have in common is feathers, and they have been around for a long time. Early protofeathers appeared in dinosaurs like *KULINDADROMEUS*, which lived about 20 million years before Archaeopteryx existed. Later, more complicated feathers evolved on many of the two-legged, meat-eating dinosaurs: predators like *ANCHIORNIS*, *SCANSORIOPTERYX*, and, of course, Archaeopteryx.

NEOGENE
(23–2.5 MILLION YEARS AGO)

55 million years after the non-avian dinosaurs disappeared, some birds had evolved into shapes – and sizes – not seen since the Cretaceous. The flightless *PHORUSRHACIDS* and the 1.5-metre-tall *ANDALGALORNIS* were elegant hunters: light-boned apex predators who roamed the South American plains in search of prey.

QUATERNARY
(2.5 MILLION YEARS AGO – PRESENT DAY)

The evolution of birds from their dinosaur ancestors has quite a few twists and turns before we get to birds we recognise nowadays. By the Quaternary, early humans would have met flightless *MOAS* larger than horses and *HAAST'S HAWKS* large enough to grab young primates in their giant talons. As humans became expert hunters, these giant birds were either eaten by people or outcompeted by them when looking for prey.

CRETACEOUS PERIOD
(145–66 MILLION YEARS AGO)

By the Cretaceous period, many dinosaurs looked more birdlike and could fly. IBEROMESORNIS looked very similar to modern birds, although it still had teeth in its beak and claws on its wings. Many of these dinosaurs lived close to water, including the cormorant-like HESPERORNIS. Then, about ten million years before the end of the Cretaceous, the first true relatives of modern birds arrived – the NEORNITHES! They didn't have teeth and the rest of their skeletons were indistinguishable from those of birds alive today.

PALAEOGENE
(66–23 MILLION YEARS AGO)

In the aftermath of the meteorite strike that killed the large dinosaurs, early members of modern groups of birds quickly appeared: perching birds like EOZYGODACTYLUS, early owls such as BERRUORNIS and even true waterbirds like AUSTRALORNIS.

Birds wouldn't become the birds we know today until they had simplified their fingerbones and lost the long, bony tails and teeth that their ancestors possessed. But what was the first bird? Pinpointing the first of any sort of an animal is a tricky thing (because not many animal remains become fossils) and defining when a bird is a real, true, actual bird is a proper head-scratcher. What we do know is that *Archaeopteryx* was just one of a HUGE number of feathered dinosaurs, and it definitely wasn't the earliest of these.

VELOCIRAPTOR WAS THE LAST RAPTOR

The word 'raptor' might make you think of VELOCIRAPTORS, the curved-clawed, two-legged dinosaurs from the Mesozoic era. But before those famous predators were discovered and named, 'raptor' meant just one thing: bird of prey. So, while *Velociraptors* are long gone, other raptors have stuck around . . .

Raptors are 'hypercarnivores' – birds whose diets are made up of over 70 per cent meat – who either hunt their prey or feed on dead animals they discover. They are found all over the world today, come in a range of elegant shapes and sizes, and hunt in ways evolved to best suit their habitats . . .

Most people tend to think of the *Accipitriformes* as the classic birds of prey: this group includes sharp-eyed predators such as the EURASIAN SPARROWHAWK, broad-winged hunters like the PHILIPPINE EAGLE, medium-sized raptors such as BLACK-BREASTED BUZZARDS, MISSISSIPPI KITES and LONG-WINGED HARRIERS, as well as African vultures like the HOODED VULTURE.

Osprey

OSPREYS are oddballs that don't quite fit in with the rest of the *Accipitriformes*. They are found in all continents except Antarctica and capture fish by snatching them from just under the water's surface. Their feet are covered in backward-facing, spike-like scales to help them hold on to slippery fish in flight.

When it comes to hunting style, the **SECRETARY BIRD** is most likely to remind you of a monster-raptor from a movie. Rather than just using their talons to hold their prey while their sharp beaks do the dirty work, these long-legged predators kick and slash at the hares, scorpions and snakes that they want to snack on.

Over in South America, the two species of **SERIEMA** live simillarly to the sub-Saharan secretary bird – slashing with their extendable, sickle-shaped toe claw on the end of their long legs to kill frogs, snakes and lizards.

The *Cathartiformes* are the South American equivalent of African vultures. Like those birds, many species of *Cathartiformes* – including the **BLACK VULTURE** and **CALIFORNIAN CONDOR** – don't have feathers around their face and neck to keep them clean when feeding on dead animals.

Large talons, sharp beaks and keen eyesight make any bird a good hunter, no matter who evolves them. Although raptors such as the **COMMON KESTREL** or **LAUGHING FALCON** look a lot like *Accipitriformes*, they are actually more closely related to parrots and songbirds than to hawks or eagles.

Far from raptors being an extinct group of predators, these modern-day dinosaurs are a diverse collection of high-speed hunters, feathered fish-eaters and low-kicking killers.

BIRDS THAT LOOK ALIKE ARE ALWAYS RELATED

WRONG! Focus your birdwatching binoculars and you will notice birds with similar names, shapes or colours turning up again and again, no matter where in the world you are. Are all these birds part of the same family? Well, while some birds might share a name or look similar, they are NOT always related . . .

Let's use robins as an example. In Europe, they are often thought of as small, round, red-bibbed winter companions. But the name 'robin' is also used for many small, round birds in Australia, such as the vibrantly coloured *PINK ROBIN*, the elegant *WHITE-WINGED ROBIN* and the common *SCARLET ROBIN*. Despite their shape and name, these species are only very distantly related to their European namesakes. In North America, the 'robin' is actually a kind of thrush – part of the same family of birds as the *EUROPEAN BLACKBIRD*.

The same is true for magpies. Although Europeans and Australians both use this word, the birds they use it for are not closely related at all! The Australian animal was named 'magpie' after European explorers saw it and thought it looked similar to their magpies back home. In fact, it had already been given other names, including 'kirayi' and 'murnubbarr', by Indigenous peoples of Australia thousands of years before. Early European settlers did the same thing when naming the *AUSTRALIAN BRUSHTURKEY*, a flightless bird that looks similar to the American *WILD TURKEY*.

Although it seems lazy of European travellers to have reused the names of similar-looking birds from their home countries on animals they were seeing for the first time, these examples tell us something interesting about the evolution of birds in different places.

Many of the birds that explorers saw were completely unrelated but HAD evolved to look like each other due to living similar lives. There are only so many environments for birds to live in, so it's not always surprising that they can adapt the same way. For example, the *ORANGE-BREASTED SUNBIRD* from Africa and the *GREEN-CROWNED BRILLIANT* from the Americas both have straw-like beaks for accessing tasty nectar. Despite being unrelated and living on different continents, they have developed similar beaks to more easily eat the same type of food.

Orange-breasted sunbird

Green-crowned brilliant

Unrelated animals evolve into similar-looking shapes to answer the same key evolutionary questions, like "How do I hide from predators?" or "How do I eat that?". This process is called 'convergent evolution' and explains how birds we call 'vultures' can be found eating the carcasses of animals in Africa as well as thousand of kilometres away in South America.

BIRDS' SUPER-SIGHT IS THEIR STRONGEST SENSE [WRONG!]

Whether it's scoping out a particularly tasty-looking snack or dodging wayward branches during a high-speed pursuit, birds have a lot to thank their eyes for. But there's a lot more going on in the sense department than it might seem . . .

Birds do have an incredible sense of sight, with 'tetrachromatic' eyes that allow them to see parts of the colour spectrum that humans can't see. When birds like **RED-BREASTED NUTHATCHES** are speeding through forests, they can see ultraviolet light reflecting off plants, making leaves easier to see and avoid. The light also reflects off urine trails left by small mammals, meaning raptors like **GREY KESTRELS** can follow glowing landing strips to their next meal.

But sight isn't the only way to make sense of your world – and some species follow their nose! Scientists once thought birds had a rubbish sense of smell, but recent research has shown that they have a fantastic 'olfactory system' (that's their noses and the part of the brain that decodes smelly signals). The part of the brain that understands smells is HUGE in seabirds like **GREAT SHEARWATERS**, probably to help them sniff out the fishiest parts of the ocean.

Some birds, like **LITTLE SPOTTED KIWIS** and **GREAT-EARED NIGHTJARS**, have whiskers that they use to detect prey by touch (when it's near their mouth) but hearing is the most important sense for other species.

Most birds, including *EURASIAN BLACKBIRDS* and *AMERICAN ROBINS*, are able to hear worms and insects under the ground or in leaf litter, but some species take listening to a new level.

Bouncing off a *BARN OWL*'s huge, heart-shaped face, the sound of a vole scratching in the undergrowth is directed into the owl's ears. The owl's outer ears are at different heights on either side of their head, which helps them locate where the sound is coming from. Inside each ear, sound is received by the 'cochlea', a curved tube containing special hairs.

Barn owl

Owl skull

Outer ear

Cochlea

In *BARN OWLS*, this tube is ENORMOUS and gives them incredibly sensitive hearing. The hairs on the cochlea react to sound vibrations and send a signal to the owl's brain, allowing it to pinpoint its prey with extraordinary, deadly accuracy.

Whichever sense is actually their most super, birds have a whole load of incredible tools at their disposal to help them make sense of the world around them.

FLYING IS EASY

In Earth's entire history, flying has only evolved a few times. Birds may make it LOOK easy, but being able to flap wings up and down is super unusual. In animals with backbones, only *Pterodactyls*, birds and bats have discovered the secret to pushing themselves up into the air.

Birds need GIGANTIC muscles to push huge amounts of air downwards and backwards to stay airborne. Two sets of muscles create the enormous power needed for flight and they both connect to a large pointy part of the bird's chest bone called the 'keel'.

Both sets of muscles have horrible, complex names: the 'pectoralis' muscles pull the wings downwards while the (deep breath) 'supracoracoideus' muscles heave the wings back upwards. These muscles are so amazingly powerful that together they can weigh from one quarter to over a third of a bird's entire weight!

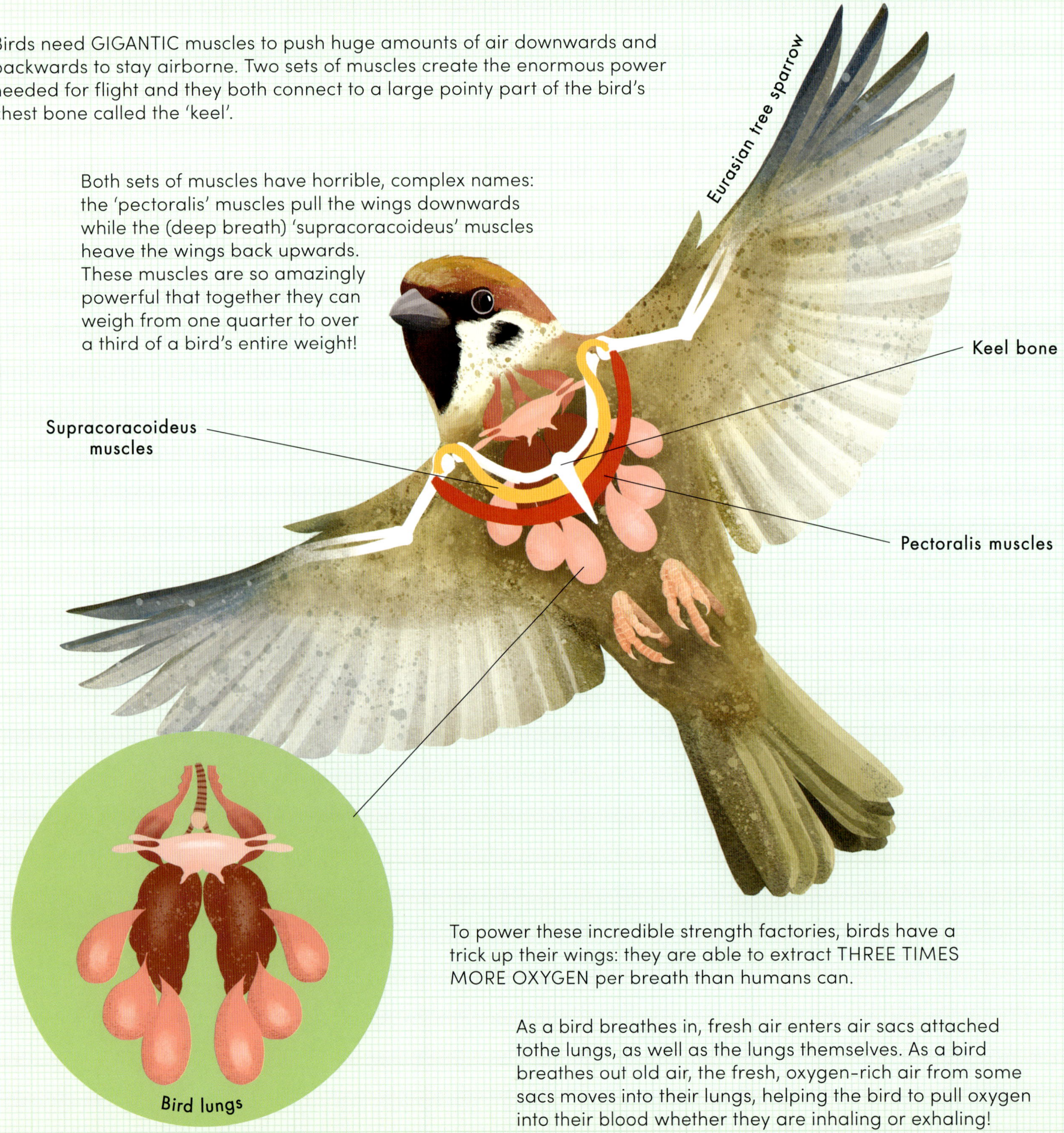

Eurasian tree sparrow

Keel bone

Supracoracoideus muscles

Pectoralis muscles

Bird lungs

To power these incredible strength factories, birds have a trick up their wings: they are able to extract THREE TIMES MORE OXYGEN per breath than humans can.

As a bird breathes in, fresh air enters air sacs attached to the lungs, as well as the lungs themselves. As a bird breathes out old air, the fresh, oxygen-rich air from some sacs moves into their lungs, helping the bird to pull oxygen into their blood whether they are inhaling or exhaling!

From **STREAKED SHEARWATERS** climbing up trees to make exhausting lift-offs easier, to **GOLDEN EAGLES** coasting on gusts of warm air called 'thermals', birds have come up with pretty smart flying behaviours. But flying is such hard work that some birds have given it up entirely.

This can happen when birds arrive on islands with different predators and gradually lose the need to fly away from danger. The **GALAPAGOS CORMORANT** has stubby wings which are now useless for flying, while the New Caledonian **KAGU** mainly uses its long wing feathers to show off.

New Zealand is a flightless-bird-spotter's paradise, with many species living mostly on the ground. The five species of adorable kiwi evolved on the islands before humans introduced predators, and act more like hedgehogs than birds. Kiwis snuffle around the undergrowth sniffing out insects, their tiny wings completely hidden beneath their fur-like feathers. Even if they tried to fly, their skeleton no longer has the important bumps and knobs that their flight muscles need to attach to.

Okarito brown kiwi

We all know flying is GREAT, but birds need to use over seven times as much energy to do it than a mammal running the same distance. They just make it LOOK effortless.

BIRDS ARE UNCLEAN

A lot of people seem to think that birds (especially city birds) are 'dirty'. Sure, city-living can be a bit hard on birds like pigeons – it's tough to stay looking sharp in busy places filled with people and pollution – but all types of birds throughout the world take their cleanliness very seriously indeed. Their lives depend on it!

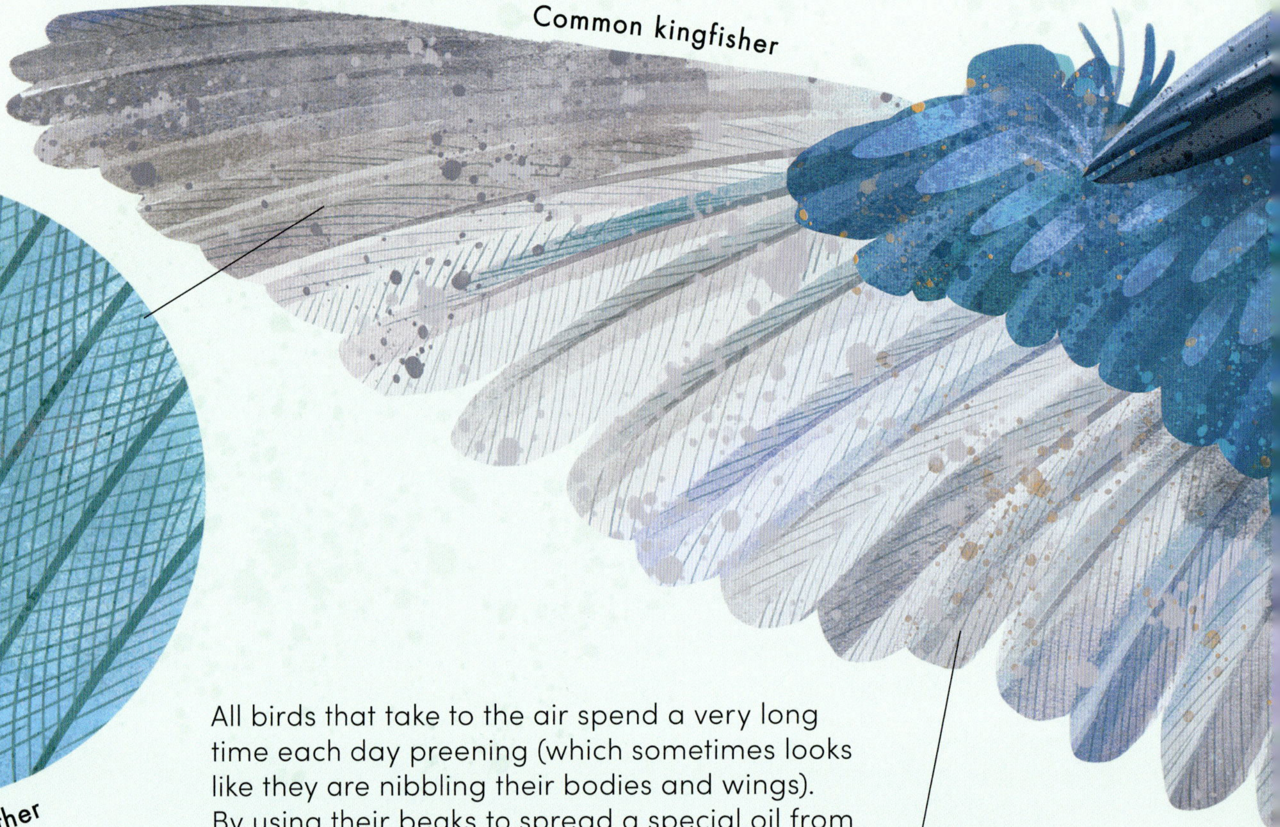

Common kingfisher

Close-up of a feather

All birds that take to the air spend a very long time each day preening (which sometimes looks like they are nibbling their bodies and wings). By using their beaks to spread a special oil from their 'uropygial' or 'preen' gland over their bodies, they help keep their feathers strong, clean and waterproofed.

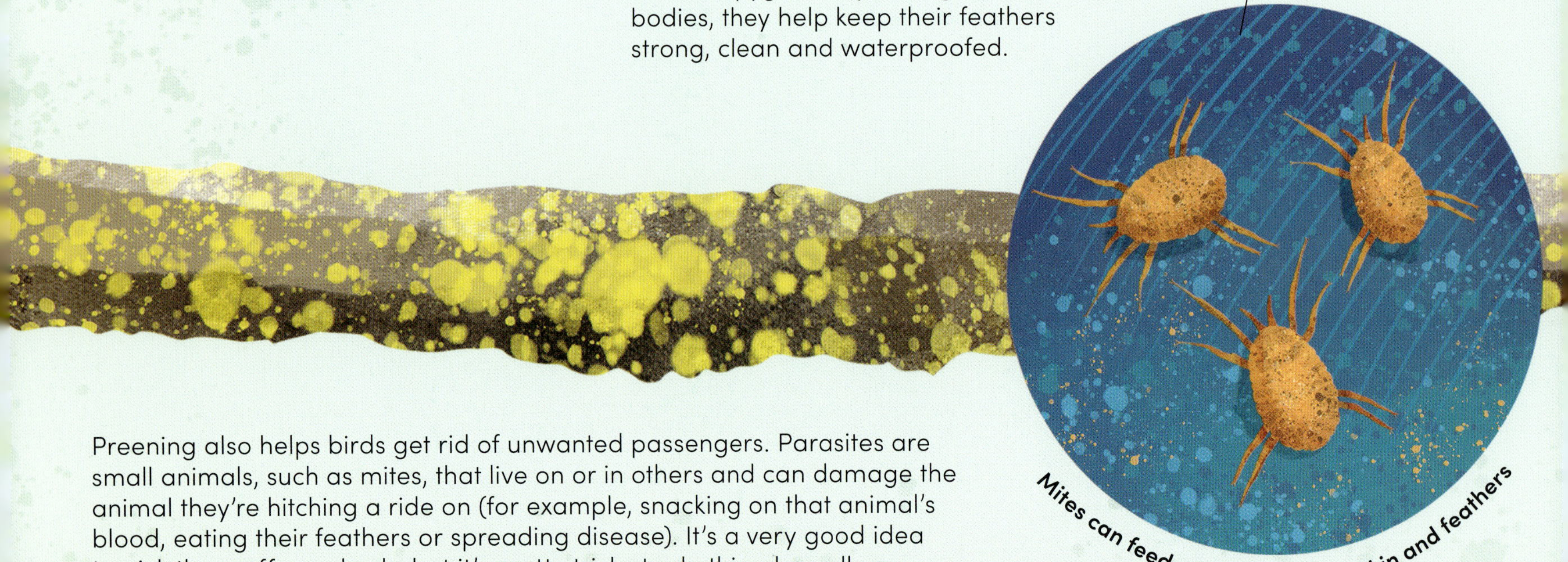

Preening also helps birds get rid of unwanted passengers. Parasites are small animals, such as mites, that live on or in others and can damage the animal they're hitching a ride on (for example, snacking on that animal's blood, eating their feathers or spreading disease). It's a very good idea to pick them off your body, but it's pretty tricky to do this when all you can use is a pair of tweezers on the front of your face.

Mites can feed on a bird's blood, skin and feathers

California quail

Some birds take baths to keep their feathers clean, but water can be hard to find in hot, dry parts of the world. The CALIFORNIA QUAIL takes a dip in dirt by kicking up clouds of dusty soil to protect their feathers from damage and smother parasites. Birds like COCKATIELS can even create their own dust, called 'dander'!

Cockatiel

Birds need their feathers to help them fly, stay warm, attract mates and hide from predators. So, it shouldn't be surprising that birds are quite the perfectionists when it comes to keeping them clean!

BIRDS ARE DEFENCELESS

To a whole heap of animals, birds are the perfect snack: parcels of super-nutritious muscle without any annoying armour that might get stuck in a predator's throat. There's not much birds can do to stop themselves from becoming a meal, at least that's what you might think . . .

We all know that leggy **OSTRICHES** bury their heads in the ground when they spot danger, hoping it'll just go away. Except . . . OF COURSE THEY DON'T! Sure, ostriches poke their heads into their ground-nests to check on their eggs, and sometimes lie down to hide when they sense danger. But when they're under real physical threat from a leopard or hyena, they use their speed! Pounding the ground with their spring-like feet, they travel the length of an alligator (over three metres) with each stride, outrunning almost anything that tries to grab a bite.

FULMAR chicks have strong stomachs when it comes to danger – they grow up on rocky ledges hundreds of metres above surging seas. But very young chicks can't fly away from hungry **SKUAS**. Instead, fulmer chicks coming face to face with predators respond by vomiting oil all over them! Being covered in bright orange oil is unpleasant enough to put most predators off, but the oil can also make a skua's feathers lose their waterproofing. Definitely something you want to avoid if you're a seabird!

PIPING PLOVERS use pretty sensational acting skills to protect their eggs. If a curious fox comes sauntering over to their nest, the parent plover will limp away, dragging their broken wing behind them. This makes them an easy meal for the agile fox and much more interesting than a nest of eggs. But the plovers are faking their injury! Parents lure the predator away from their unborn young, only to flap to safety when snapping jaws get too close.

Piping plover

One of the most surprising bird defences has only recently been discovered. The **HOODED PITOHUI** from South America and the **BLUE-CAPPED IFRITA** from New Guinea are two of only a handful of known poisonous bird species. These brightly coloured birds become poisonous from snacking on beetles in the undergrowth. Not only do their beautiful feathers warn predators to stay away, but the poison (which just so happens to be the same sort that is found in notorious poison dart frogs) is carried IN the feathers themselves.

From clever tricks to poisoned feathers, birds have far too many ingenious defences to just bury their heads in the sand and hope that danger goes away . . .

ALL BIRDS EAT SEEDS

So, yes, OK, some species of birds do enjoy a diet of tasty seeds. Ducks like *MALLARDS* and *SMEWS* have bills that are just right for gobbling them up off the surface of the water, while *BLUE TITS* and *CHAFFINCHES* just LOVE hanging out at their local neighbourhood birdfeeders.

But seeds are only ONE type of food that birds like to nibble. Different bird species eat an enormous array of things and, just like ducks, their beaks have adapted to help them find, catch and eat all these types of food.

VAMPIRE GROUND FINCHES nibble parasites off other birds, then use their sharp beaks to pierce the animal's skin and drink the blood around the wound.

BEE-EATERS catch bees and wasps in mid-air and use their long, tweezer-like beaks to squeeze the venom out of their lunch.

The chunky beak of the South American **HOATZIN** is great for ripping leaves and flowers off tropical trees. They digest their food slowly, which creates a lot of gas (this is why they're also called 'stinkbirds')!

BUTCHERBIRDS eat insects but also use their powerful beaks to skewer lizards on thorns for safekeeping, returning to devour them later.

The *LILAC-BREASTED ROLLER* enjoys a very impressive diet of venomous centipedes, scorpions and even snakes!

FLAMINGOS use horny plates in their beaks to filter tiny invertebrates from shallow water as they swish it into and out of their mouths.

SPOONBILLS sway their long beaks from side to side under the surface of fresh water, snapping up any crustaceans or fish that their spatula-like bill detects.

The enormous, sharp-ended beak of the *SHOEBILL* is excellent for capturing huge prey, including lungfish and even baby crocodiles!

YELLOW-BELLIED SUNBIRD-ASITY insert their long beaks deep into flowers to reach the energy-rich nectar inside.

BEARDED VULTURES are one of the few animals that eat the bones of their prey rather than the meat, relying on powerful stomach acid to break down the bones for digestion.

No matter what their snack of choice, birds rely on their beaks to help them crunch, snip, pierce or smash their way to a full stomach.

OWLS ONLY COME OUT AT NIGHT

It's true that a lot of owls prefer to hunt under the cover of true darkness – zoologists call species with this preference 'nocturnal'. BUT almost 25 per cent of all owl species are 'crepuscular': they are most active at dawn and dusk, when there's a little light in the sky.

Let's take a moment to think about what amazing predators owls are. Their giant eyes let them see by the tiny light of the moon and the stars. Their outer ears sit at different heights on either side of their head, helping them zero in on the quietest footprints. Even their feathers are special: the fluffy edges break up the air, stopping telltale WHOOSH-ing sounds and making the birds deathly silent as they glide towards their prey.

Spectacled owl

All this makes owls' bodies super killing machines, beautifully adapted for hunting by surprise. You won't find crepuscular owls patrolling the skies at midnight, but their huge eyes and incredible hearing still give them an advantage over their prey.

Some owls actually don't hunt at night at all – these species are 'diurnal'. **NORTHERN PYGMY OWLS** are small and camouflaged, blending into the trees they hunt from. Although they are incredible hunters, they need to avoid becoming another raptor's lunch, and have two eye spots on the back of their heads to scare off attackers.

In fact, some owls don't even mind if it's the middle of the night or the middle of the afternoon. **SNOWY OWLS** hunt during the night, but also during the day, when they rely on their incredible snow-white camouflage to sneak up on lemmings and Arctic hares.

Although nocturnal owls are the most famous night-time birds, they're not alone in the dark. **SRI LANKA FROGMOUTHS** look a lot like owls and hunt at night, but they are actually cousins of hummingbirds. They rely on their keen vision and the bristly whiskers around their beaks to detect insects in flight, which they gobble up in their enormous mouths.

Beautiful **BLACK-CROWNED NIGHT HERONS** live much like their diurnal relatives by preying on other animals, while **NIGHTJARS** like the **COMMON POORWILL** tumble around the sky, hunting for moths and drinking from rivers and lakes without landing.

Even the world's largest parrot – the **KĀKĀPŌ** – sings its lonely mating call at night, echoing around the mountains of New Zealand under the stars.

So, the next time you hear an owl's screech in the night, have a really close listen. It could just be a diurnal owl having a bad dream . . .

BIRDSONG SOUNDS LOVELY

Ah, birdsong: trills and melodies that have inspired poets and musicians for thousands of years. But birds make sounds for each other, not for people, and not all birdsong is beautiful to human ears. . .

Some birds can sound like other animals: humans often mistake a **COMMON LOON** for a wolf when it opens its beak, while the **GREEN CATBIRD** sounds something like a baby crying mixed with a very unhappy cat . . .

The spooky, moan-like calls of the giant-eyed **GREAT POTOO** echo around the pitch-black forests of Central America as it hunts small animals like lizards through the night. No wonder it is known as the 'ghost bird'!

Other birds can sound, well, annoying. Australian **BELL MINERS** aren't easy to spot because of their leaf-coloured, camouflaged feathers, but thanks to their endless pinging calls, they are impossible to ignore!

Lots of birds that live in tropical forests – like the unbelievably loud **WHITE BELLBIRDS** and the screaming **NANDAY CONURES** of South America – have short, sharp, loud calls. Longer, more intricate songs would simply get muffled, reflected off shiny leaves hanging on the thousands of trees around them.

For every deafening bellbird, there is a *BUSH WARBLER*, sweetly decorating the air with a beautiful tune. But the hiss of a *TURKEY VULTURE* and the sweet chirps of a *NIGHTINGALE* are actually very similar when we think about what these signals really mean. Even delightful chirrups have an ugly side . . .

Nightingale

Turkey vulture

The majority of bird calls mean one of two things: "Here I am, aren't I great?" or "Get out of here!". You can hear both of these together if you're up early enough to hear the 'dawn chorus', when hundreds of birds sing their hearts out at the first morning light. Although humans might think our feathered neighbours are whistling good morning to each other, they are actually pumped-up males warning others birds to stay away and trying to show off to females they want to have chicks with.

Brown-headed cowbird

With birds like *BROWN-HEADED COWBIRDS* taking two years to perfect their songs, and over 15 per cent of birds being able to sing in duets, there's no doubt birdsong is an impressive feat of evolution. But don't be fooled – those cheery cheeps are a lot grumpier than they might sound to our human ears.

BIRDS CAN SPEAK

WRONG!

"Polly want a cracker?" It's an excellent question but it's unlikely that any parrot that manages to say this sentence actually understands what they're asking – no matter how chatty they are. They might not even like crackers . . .

Many species of parrots kept by humans can copy (or, to use the scientific word, 'mimic') words and phrases they hear their owners repeating. One *GREY PARROT* called Alex was trained by scientists to use over 100 words! Indian *ROSE-RINGED PARAKEETS* have been kept as pets to show off their skills of repetition for hundreds of years, a habit that might have started when the birds picked up religious chants they heard repeated in sacred temples.

Rose-ringed parakeet

Common hill myna

It's not just pirate playmates that can copy human speech. The *COMMON HILL MYNA* is a famous mimic of human sounds, while European species such as starlings have been trained to strain their vocal organs to repeat complex phrases from many languages.

Learning to 'say' certain phrases in order to receive rewards is what scientists call 'operant conditioning', but it isn't really the bird speaking with words it understands . . .

Over 300 species of birds can mimic the sounds, calls and cries made by other species – not just humans. It's an impressive number considering mimicry is incredibly hard to do! In fact, all the birds that can mimic have one thing in common: they have very large brains.

The **SUPERB LYREBIRD** has a powerful brain that is particularly large in comparison to its body size. This explains how they can listen, remember and then mimic many other birds they share their home with, as well as human noises like camera clicks and car alarms. They can even learn the songs of other species of birds from other lyrebirds.

Superb lyrebird

Kookaburra

We know why birds sing (see page 24), but why do some birds mix other species' chatter into their own song? Ornithologists are still trying to answer this, but as good mimicry means a massive brain, the birds might be advertising their intelligence to possible mates.

Some birds might have evolved mimicry for very clever reasons indeed. **PIED CURRAWONGS** eat **BROWN THORNBILL** chicks – so when thornbills see currawongs near a nest, they mimic the alarm calls of **NEW HOLLAND HONEYEATERS**. Honeyeaters alert other birds when a **BROWN GOSHAWK** is around: a predator even the currawong would want to hide from. By making the currawong flee from a goshawk (which isn't there!), the thornbills buy themselves time to escape to safety. Smart!

Pied currawong

Brown thornbill

Whatever the reason for it, mimicry in birds is generally about getting something, like safety from a pied currawong . . . or a treat from an owner.

WRONG!

PEOPLE THINK ALL BIRDS ARE BEAUTIFUL

Birds have a reputation for being beautiful. For at least 12,000 years, we humans have drawn birds on cave walls and coffee cups, and have even imagined gods in their image. This is a bit odd – birds don't need to look attractive to humans, just to each other. Some birds don't line up with what most humans consider to be 'beautiful', but how they look is still important . . .

SOUTHERN GROUND HORNBILL

This metre-long, monkey-eating *HORNBILL* isn't going to win any beauty pageants, but its bright red wattle (loose skin on its neck) helps it make its booming, roar-like call.

JAVAN FROGMOUTH

JAVAN FROGMOUTHS have dull brown feathers, but these help them blend in with nearby tree branches to cleverly avoid being caught by predators.

GREATER ADJUTANT

The *GREATER ADJUTANT* is unusual looking, but their bald head prevents their feathers getting messy when they stick their heads into animal flesh. Less than 1,000 of these storks remain in the wild today.

TURKEY VULTURE

Using the same evolutionary trick as the greater adjutant, *TURKEY VULTURES* lack feathers on their red heads so that they can easily plunge their beaks into the rotting corpses of dead animals.

NORTHERN BALD IBIS

The wrinkled, bare-skinned face of the *NORTHERN BALD IBIS* doesn't win it many human fans, but this large species is endangered. With less than 800 individuals living in the wild, these birds need our help.

MUSCOVY DUCK

The peculiar red bulging cushions surrounding a *MUSCOVY DUCK*'s beak are more practical than pretty: they release an oil that can weatherproof the duck's feathers.

Birds don't need to look good to humans to survive in their environments. In fact, not 'looking good' might be a helpful thing for them. Many birds are endangered and although this is mainly due to habitat destruction (see page 54), for many years 'beautiful' species were hunted by humans so they could get their hands on the birds' stunning feathers.

Egret feather
Pacific reef heron feather
Peacock feather
Emu feather
Ostrich feather
Lyrebird feather

Cultures all over the world have decorated their clothes and headgear with bird feathers for thousands of years, but Europeans in the 18th and 19th centuries took this to an extreme.

Ear tufts from **GREAT CRESTED GREBES** were so sought after in Europe that in the late 19th century there were just over 80 birds of that species left in the entire UK. Egrets, herons, parrots . . . many birds were facing extinction around the world, just because of human fashion.

Great crested grebe

By the end of the nineteenth century, Emily Williamson and Eliza Phillips in the UK and Harriet Hemenway in the USA, along with others, began to campaign to stop the damage. Their efforts eventually created the RSPB in the UK and Audubon in the USA – charities that help protect birds around the world, no matter how 'beautiful' humans think they are.

IT'S EASY FOR BIRDS TO FIND A PARTNER

Like lots of other animals, birds need to find themselves a mate in order to have a family of chicks and keep their species going. But proving that you would make a perfect partner isn't easy . . .

Some birds use their appearance to their advantage – species such as the **GREAT ARGUS** have stunning plumage that they can use to impress. The more interesting shapes these birds make with their long and colourful feathers, the more exciting they look to other birds of their species! Some birds even sport feathers that can't be used for flying – they just exist to help them look good.

Other birds twin their feathers with *spectacular* dance moves. The **RED-CAPPED MANAKIN** pairs its bright yellow legs with a brilliant, energetic performance. Effortlessly sliding sideways and backwards along branches, it wows nearby females with a complicated series of movements – including one that looks like the human 'moonwalk'!

MAGNIFICENT RIFLEBIRDS and **GREATER BIRD-OF-PARADISE** also bob, stretch and twirl to show off. **VOGELKOP LOPHORINA** even clear a stage so they don't trip over any stray twigs! The more complex the bird's performance, the more attention it gets.

It's not just dancing that birds use to prove themselves. Around 15 species of birds across Australia and New Guinea impress by building amazing towers and arches (called 'bowers') out of objects they find in their forest homes. The *VOGELKOP BOWERBIRD* builds incredible cone-shaped huts decorated with stones, moss, flowers and beetle cases, while *SATIN BOWERBIRDS* mostly decorate with objects made of blue plastic!

Vogelkop bowerbird

These bowers can sometimes look like nests, but they aren't used for shelter. The building process is watched closely by female bowerbirds who judge the finished structures, and it seems that bowerbirds build them purely to show off the art they can create.

From flexible feathers and daring dancing to creative displays of bower-building, birds have a lot of ways to impress each other. Whichever method they use, it's hard work for birds to win over a partner . . .

DODOS WERE SILLY

Dodos were silly, short-legged birds that clumsily tripped into extinction after Dutch sailors landed on the island of Mauritius in the sixteenth century. Right?

Well . . . the story of the dodo is a little bit more complicated. For starters, they weren't clumsy. They actually had very strong, long, muscular legs for hiking up and down the mountainous terrain of their home – not unlike those of today's *TAKAHĒS*.

By studying preserved dodo DNA, experts now know that dodos evolved from a type of *PIGEON* that found the island millions of years before the sailors did. Over time, the pigeon's ancestors became larger, stockier and more powerful.

Takahē

The dodo had been inaccurately described for decades because no one realised that the species was becoming extinct. No one was interested in collecting the birds for science at the time, and only a few sketches from life were ever made. The image of the useless dodo that we know today was created by artists working at least 100 years after the last dodo had died!

Dodo

So, dodos didn't look exactly like we have all been told they did. But did they cause their own extinction?

No! Dodos weren't stupid – they actually had quite large brains – but they were naive. Because they hadn't met humans before, they didn't realise that they might be dangerous to investigate. After all, dodos had evolved on an island where they had no natural predators. They had even lost the ability to fly because there was no need to escape from anything.

The sailors who arrived on Mauritius in 1598 just scooped them up, threw them in their cooking pots and ate them all, right? Well, while visitors did eat some of the birds, letters and diaries written by the sailors show that dodos didn't actually taste that good!

Instead, the dodo's demise was because of other animals those sailors brought with them to the island: pigs and rats. These mammals quickly discovered the dodos' eggs, which had been laid on the ground one at a time. The introduction of these 'invasive species' meant the dodos soon had their eggs stolen and eaten faster than they could replace them. Only 60 years after the first humans, pigs and rats arrived on Mauritius, the dodo had disappeared forever.

We'll never know exactly what dodos looked like, but the idea that the dodo was a silly animal whose foolishness caused it to die out should definitely become extinct.

SEAGULLS ARE MEAN

First off, THERE'S NO SUCH THING AS A SEAGULL. Sure, gulls like the *BLACK-HEADED GULL* and the *CASPIAN GULL* spend time around coasts: their webbed feet are perfect for paddling and they have a taste for fish.

But 'seagull' is just a name people use to talk about the fifty-odd species of gulls that live on Earth. From the white-feathered, blue-beaked *IVORY GULL* living at the very northernmost parts of the Arctic Circle to the *GREY GULL* that prefers to breed in the extremely dry Atacama Desert, far away from the nearest water, it seems like these birds are everywhere.

People never seem to have nice things to say about gulls, no matter which species they are talking about. They're a menace, their behaviour is out of control and their rampage must be stopped! But do gulls deserve their dastardly reputation?

Gulls are like other birds and will defend their chicks if a threat – or what they think might be a threat – gets too close to their little ones. Any human that veers too close to a young gull can expect an angry display of outstretched wings and a whole heap of screeching from the adult looking after it. That's just good parenting!

The popular idea is that gulls are vicious food thieves who will attack humans. Well, gulls actually eat a lot of different foods, from plants and worms to moles! Occasionally, they can behave like 'kleptoparasites', meaning they will sometimes let other animals find food before they swoop in and steal it. If a gull sees a delicious sandwich being held loosely, they might take their chance! But their target is not the hands holding the food.

Stealing food from others might seem mean, but gulls need big brains to do it. In 2023, scientists studying **HERRING GULLS** found that the birds watched humans to decide what to eat! If a human enjoyed something, the birds decided that it probably tasted good.

Gulls made their homes in areas long before they became towns or beachfronts. Maybe it's a bit rude of us not to offer them our food. After all, they were here first . . .

BIRDWATCHERS JUST WATCH BIRDS WRONG!

Birdwatchers watch a lot of birds. That's obvious. But that isn't the only thing that they do. In fact, people who are REALLY interested in studying birds might not call themselves birdwatchers at all: they are 'ornithologists' and do a whole lot of stuff on top of peering through binoculars.

One of the most important things ornithologists do is 'ringing'. After catching birds in mist nets (very light, almost invisible nets that don't harm the animals in them), a metal or plastic ring is carefully placed around a bird's leg. If that bird is photographed or caught months or years later, the code on the ring helps the ornithologist work out how far the bird may have migrated, its age and how healthy it is.

Other bird scientists watch and listen for evidence that certain birds are living in a specific area. By learning where species live and what they need to survive, experts can help protect birds' environments from being damaged by humans.

But ornithologists don't have to spend all their time outside. Some bird scientists prefer to explore the past by searching for extinct species in fossil records, while others spend their days performing experiments in laboratories.

Some ornithologists are interested in how birds manage to move in perfect coordination without crashing into each other. They try to work that out using extremely complicated maths that recreates murmurations inside computer programmes – thousands of individual birds all swooping and sweeping in a digital sky.

Other bird experts want to learn how birds experience the world. They use special cameras to peer into a spectrum of colours that humans can't see, hoping to get a birds-eye view of flowers, eggs and the feathers of other birds.

Ornithologists interested in flight can't study birds up in the clouds. Instead, they use wind tunnels. By watching how gas and air move over bird-shaped models, the scientists get a much better idea of how real birds are able to speed through the sky.

People who study birds might not call themselves the same thing – they might think of themselves as ornithologists, biologists, ecologists or teachers. Whatever they call themselves, they'd all agree on this: studying birds can involve a lot more than simply watching them.

BIRDWATCHING ISN'T FOR EVERYONE WRONG!

A lot of people think birdwatching is a boring hobby for grown-ups. But birdwatchers can be any age, from anywhere. The great thing about birdwatching is that, because birds are found all over the world, there is no limit to the kind of person that can enjoy doing it!

JEFFREY WARD

Jeffrey lives in Texas, USA, and teaches people as a bird guide both on walks and online. He has seen over 400 types of birds in North America, and loves playing basketball.

MYA-ROSE CRAIG

Mya-Rose is a British-Bangladeshi birder and activist. By the time she was 17, she had already seen half of the world's birds species! Today, she inspires people to learn about the natural world.

ÁLVARO LUNA

Álvaro is a Spanish scientist researching how birds survive when their homes are polluted. He loves taking photographs, particularly of Pampas, Argentina.

LAUREN PHARR

Lauren is a scientist from North Carolina, USA, who studies how changes to climate alter birds' behaviour. Her favourite bird is the *RED-COCKADED WOODPECKER*.

LIRA VALENCIA

Lira is a ranger at Walthamstow Wetlands in London, UK, where she educates people about the amazing birds – and other nature – found there.

ALYSSA J. SARGENT

Alyssa uses tiny tracking devices to research how hummingbirds behave in Colombia. She also likes boxing and writing fantasy fiction!

CHITI ARVIND

Chiti is an Indian scientist who is examining how birds like *WHITE-BELLIED SHOLAKILIS* talk to each other. In her spare time, Chiti loves backpacking and baking.

ELOISE HUNT

Eloise is an ornithologist from Norfolk, UK. She studies the evolution of birds by looking at their fossils, and she loves vintage fashion!

INDIGO GOODSON-FIELDS

Indigo is a writer and poet living in New York, USA. She fell in love with birds in 2020 and now mixes poetry with birdwatching in her local green spaces.

BADGER WETHERHILL

Badger is a Scottish birder who originally trained as a botanist. His favourite place that he has looked for birds is Christmas Island, in the Indian Ocean.

MURRY BURGESS

Murry is an American professor who studies birds in towns and cities. She also loves playing video games and snuggling with her dog, Loki!

SABRINA SCHALZ

Sabrina is a German scientist studying the ways birds and humans listen to each other. She loves birding with her baby and growing her wildlife-friendly garden.

SORREL LYALL

Sorrel is an English ornithologist who works to protect birds and teach young people about them. In her spare time, she enjoys painting wildlife with watercolours.

JOSEFA SCHERRER

Josefa is a scientist from Tennessee, USA, who makes tiny microscopes to watch how bird neurons flash when they sing! They love building things that help people understand science.

ANAÏS DUHAMEL

Anaïs is a French scientist who studies ancient birds. She has been bird spotting in the Amazon, fossil hunting on Saint Helena Island, and enjoys drawing the birds she studies.

JAROME ALI

Jarome is a scientist from Trinidad and Tobago who studies how and why birds like parrots evolved to be so colourful. Jarome has been bitten by hedgehogs and roared at by wild lionesses in the field!

LOUISA MAMALIS

Louisa is a conservation scientist who works to protect the *GIANT IBIS*, a Critically Endangered bird from Cambodia. Lou also loves plants and is a long-distance runner!

PENGUINS ONLY LIVE AT THE SOUTH POLE WRONG!

One of the biggest bird blunders is when penguins show up on Christmas cards. Father Christmas – as you may know – lives up in the Arctic Circle, but all penguins live near the South Pole on the opposite side of the world! Well, that's almost right. Although penguins are a southern hemisphere species, none of them really live at the South Pole itself. That place is far too far away from the sea for an animal that eats fish!

So, maybe penguins don't live right at the South Pole, but they all live in Antarctica, right? Well . . . no. CHINSTRAP, MACARONI and GENTOO PENGUINS do visit the northernmost tip of Antarctica's peninsula to breed, but it's only ADELIE and EMPEROR PENGUINS that live there all year round.

The seas around Antarctica are full of life and make superb hunting grounds for fish fans. But don't be fooled – it is a super-hard place to live, with incredible cold and terrible wind. And it certainly isn't the only place penguins live.

KING PENGUINS might look a lot like emperors, but they're found in much more northern areas than their larger cousins. Almost a million of these noisy birds can be found breeding on the Crozet Islands, about halfway between Antarctica and Africa.

Over on the other side of the frozen continent, jazzy-looking *SNARES PENGUINS* live around the Snares Islands, just south of New Zealand. These penguins nest in cosy colonies under trees in the Olearia forest – not a hint of ice anywhere! *LITTLE PENGUINS* also enjoy warmer New Zealand temperatures, nesting in burrows along the coastline.

GALAPAGOS PENGUINS live on the Galapagos Islands, 960 kilometres west of Ecuador. Temperatures can reach 30 degrees Celsius in the wet season, although the waters around the islands remain quite cool. To deal with the heat on land, Galapagos penguins carry less fat and have fewer feathers on their small bodies than their larger, cold-weather cousins.

The largest Galapagos island sits right ON the equator, so any Galapagos penguins breeding on the northernmost tip are actually closer to the North Pole than the South Pole!

NESTS ARE ROUND AND MADE OF TWIGS   WRONG!

Picture a nest, and you'll probably think of a bowl made of sticks and twigs, wedged snugly in the branches of a tree. Sure, some nests look like this. But if there's one thing you know by now, it's that there are a lot of birds, and a lot of ways to do things . . .

Lots of birds don't even bother to build a nest – nests take a long time to make, and mean the bird has to go out and find stuff to build them from. In places where there are hardly any plants, birds like LITTLE AUKS and HIMALAYAN MONALS rely on small ground scrapings or stone cavities, perhaps with a few pebbles pushed around the eggs to stop them from rolling away.

When birds do build nests, they aren't all made from plants: CARIBBEAN HORNEROS build dome nests out of mud which hardens in the sun, while COMMON SWIFTS build their nests out of different materials held together with sticky saliva.

Burrowing underground is also an excellent way to keep yourself and your eggs safe, and many birds do this instead of hiding high up in a tree. PUFFINS and CHUCAO TAPACULO make long burrows, lining them with cosy materials like soft bamboo leaves, and keeping their young away from predators.

Once a bird has laid eggs in a nest, they often sit on them to transfer body warmth to the developing chicks. Chicken-lookalike MALLEEFOWLS get around this by building enormous mounds of soil and rotting leaves. The compost releases heat and keeps the chicks toasty and warm, without an adult's bottom in sight!

The smallest known nests belong to the VERVAIN HUMMINGBIRD, whose one-centimetre eggs sit in walnut-sized nests built from moss, bark and spider silk. The largest nests belong to BALD EAGLES. Their gigantic egg fortresses can weigh two tonnes, the same as a teenage African elephant!

SOCIABLE WEAVERS create apartment blocks where 500 birds can live, each featuring downward-facing entrances to protect chicks from hungry snakes. PENDULINE TIT nests can be built from grass and have two entrances – one real and one fake to guard against attacks. For extra security, the real entrance is sealed with a spiderweb-covered sticky flap: a front door!

False doors, sun-baked domes or just a few pebbles on the ground. Bird eggs can have many homes, not just the round, stick-y sort!

BIRDS AREN'T VERY SMART

Birds aren't known for being the animal kingdom's greatest thinkers. Even some of the species humans do consider smart – owls, for example – aren't quite as wise as you might have been led to believe! However, there are some birds with truly ASTONISHING brains that allow them to behave in equally astonishing ways.

Raven

From dolphins to chimpanzees, playing is one of the sure signs of animal smarts. Playing shows that birds think about complicated interactions with other animals and strengthens their brain to help them solve puzzles in later life. RAVENS have long childhoods that they spend learning through play, and as adults they still inject a lot of silliness into their days. They have even been spotted sliding down snowy hills for what looks suspiciously like fun!

Long-billed woodcreeper

A whole flock of other bird species have learned to observe other animals in order to snap up food. LONG-BILLED WOODCREEPERS follow marching ants so they can peck at any insects trying to avoid the ants, while CALIFORNIA SCRUB JAYS have brains that can store the location of hundreds of pieces of food they have hidden for the chilly winter months.

Birds of prey can even manage some complicated maths! PEREGRINE FALCONS calculate where the bird they are chasing will be at a certain moment, so that they can sneak up and launch a surprise attack.

The REAL test of whether an animal is brainy is whether it can use tools. Not screwdrivers or drills, but objects from their environment that they use to help them do certain tasks.

STRIATED HERONS use bait to catch fish, placing leaves on the surface of the water and waiting until their prey investigate the floating shape before striking.

The very best toolmaker is probably another corvid (the group of birds that includes ravens). **NEW CALEDONIAN CROWS** actually build tools, bending and shaping sticks for particular jobs and then keeping them to use again. Some tools created by these crows are so complicated that a human would have to be at least five years old to successfully make the same thing.

You can't get a much more nutrient-packed treat than insect larvae, but many of these are hidden deep inside logs. They are impossible to reach – except for **WOODPECKER FINCHES**, who snap off cactus spines and use them like spears to spike the larvae before pulling them out of their hiding places.

Maths, engineering and playtime. Birds have a lot more going on in their brains than you might have thought . . .

PIGEONS ARE PESTS WRONG!

If you visit almost any town or city on Earth, it's likely you'll spot a *FERAL PIGEON*. In fact, these grey birds are found on every continent except Antarctica, and there might be as many as 300 million of them on our planet! Some people think that members of the pigeon family are simply unwelcome depositors of poop . . . but all pigeons are AMAZING!

Pigeons are FAST! The birds you might meet on a stroll through town can easily reach speeds of up to 110 kilometres per hour. This comes in handy when they're trying to outmanoeuvre one of their many predators, like the speedy **PEREGRINE FALCON**.

There are over 300 different species of pigeons and doves (together called *Columbidae*). From the **THICK-BILLED GREEN PIGEON** to the **NICOBAR PIGEON**, members of the *Columbidae* family can be as colourful as any species of parrot. Some, like the Australian **DIAMOND DOVE**, are the size of a small sparrow, while others, like the enormous **VICTORIA CROWNED PIGEONS** of New Guinea, are as big as turkeys!

The feral pigeons that hang out in today's town squares are the great-great-grand-chicks of pigeons that were kept as pets before escaping back into the wild. These birds were once domesticated **ROCK PIGEONS**. Over thousands of years, humans kept the animals that were the most interesting to them and bred the chicks that had the longest feathers or the biggest beaks, to pass on their shapes and colours to the next generation of birds.

Feral pigeon

The way that this process happened fascinated Charles Darwin, a famous scientist and naturalist. Along with friends such as Alfred Russel Wallace, Charles was able to use domisticated pigeons and the wild birds he studied around the world to help him come up with a theory to explain how animals' looks, shape or behaviour could change over time.

Charles Darwin

Today, human understanding of everything from how different medicines effectively treat illness to how different dinosaurs were related to each other is all thanks to how we understand the incredible scientific idea that Charles and Alfred put forward: the *THEORY OF EVOLUTION*.

So, the next time you spot a pigeon when you're out and about, remind yourself how fascinating these birds and their family members truly are!

BIRDS AND PEOPLE DON'T MIX WRONG!

This is partially true – for most species, humans are bad news. They destroy habitats birds need for nesting or hunting, and have even managed to change the climate birds rely on . . . but some birds do enjoy a rare connection with humans.

Birds of prey have been kept for falconry and trained to hunt wild prey in countless cultures, for perhaps as long as 4,000 years. *SPARROWHAWKS* and other species that are kept for falconry are comfortable around their humans, but they are basically very well-trained pets that have to obey their owner's commands.

The birds that have the greatest relationship with humans are the *GREATER HONEYGUIDES*, small birds that love the taste of bee larvae, wax and honey. They know just where to find beehives in their neighbourhood, but getting inside them on their own often involves being stung.

Instead, they lead humans to the hives, trilling as they dart in front of the honey hunters. Then, when the humans have cut the hive down and opened it up, they thank their bird guide by leaving delicious wax for the honeyguide to feast on. Win-win!

The rest of the world's birds like to keep a serious distance between themselves and humans. But because we tend to build on birds' natural homes, birds either have to move away to find the ecosystems they need OR adapt to a new environment of bricks, concrete and glass.

Birds such as **FERAL PIGEONS** and **EUROPEAN STARLINGS** have done extremely well in cities – these species are found in eight out of every ten cities on Earth! But it's not just these urbanites that are found in the squares, piazzas and souks of the world. Incredibly, 20 per cent of all bird species on Earth are found in cities.

Cities have even helped one species bounce back from near-extinction. By the 1970s, **PEREGRINE FALCONS** had almost disappeared from North America due to dangerous chemicals being sprayed on crops that the birds were eating. The chemicals were eventually banned and experts stepped in to protect the species.

The experts trying to increase the falcon population worked in cities and, surprisingly, found that the urban setting was perfect for the birds: skyscrapers were just as good as cliffs for mounting attacks, and there were thousands of tasty pigeons to chase. In some areas of the USA, there are now more peregrine falcons living in cities than in the countryside.

Generally, humans and birds don't really make great pals, but at least a few species manage to get on with us despite our differences!

49

ALL BIRDS MAKE GREAT PETS

Humans have had birds as pets for over 5,000 years, from the time of the ancient Egyptians! But, despite this history, birds aren't often suited to being pets. Animals with the ability to fly don't always belong in enclosures. And taking care of birds can be pretty demanding . . .

If you DO keep a bird as a pet, it's incredibly important to be a good owner and take special note of the many things each species needs. Parakeets such as *BUDGERIGARS* are popular pets worldwide, but they need large enclosures to stretch out in, with bars quite close together so they won't get their head or feet stuck in them.

They should have access to natural sunlight (not through a window) or a full-spectrum UV lamp to help them absorb calcium from their food, different-sized perches to exercise on, and toys to keep their brain sharp and healthy.

Water dispensers and enclosures should be cleaned daily, and a budgerigar's diet needs to include a varied menu of fruits, vegetables, seeds and specially sold parakeet food. There's a lot to remember!

Although keeping birds as pets isn't as fashionable as it once was, it is still popular worldwide, with one in three households still having pet birds in some cities. Songbirds like the **BALI MYNA** are hugely sought-after pets – on the Indonesian island of Java, ornithologists think there are now more captive songbirds than there are living in the island's forests!

How do birds like these become pets? While some are born in captivity specifically to be kept by humans, the sad truth is that many are captured from their wild homes and sold, either in markets or online. This is illegal, but people want birds so badly that they are willing to pay criminals for beautiful species like **WHITE-RUMPED SHAMAS** or **SUNSET LORIKEETS**.

It's not just those bird species that are caught up in this illegal process (called 'trafficking'), but 25 per cent of ALL bird and mammal species! While this is REALLY bad news for the wild animals, keeping these species as pets can also be dangerous for their owners. Wild-caught animals can easily spread diseases like the horrible *psittacosis*, which infectious parrots only show symptoms of when they are stressed.

So, for the health and happiness of birds and the humans that love them, it's best to appreciate species through binoculars rather than keeping them in your home.

BABY BIRDS ARE ADORABLE   WRONG!

All those fluffy feathers and those big, friendly eyes . . . baby birds are just too cute! Only . . . when was the last time you really looked at a chick?

Some birds – like chickens and ducks – hatch out of their eggs ready to face the world, looking particularly sweet. But baby birds are not always the balls of cuteness you picture them being.

NIGHT-HERONS are stocky, aquatic hunters that wear their feathers, with style. But not their chicks, whose spiky, haphazardly feathered necks reach upwards out of their stick-built nests.

The North American *NORTHERN CARDINAL* sports brown and blood-red plumage and a regal head crest as an adult, but this species takes time to grow into its spectacular good looks. Chicks are born with their eyes shut tight behind bulging lids, their necks too weak to lift their head for more than a few moments, and skin so thin it is almost transparent.

These chicks, along with the chicks of almost all perching birds, from *PITTAS* to *SUNBIRDS*, are born naked and helpless and look very different to their feathery adult counterparts.

Just because some chicks don't LOOK adorable, it doesn't mean they're not sweet in nature, right? OK, chicks are ravenous eating machines that bully their parents into feeding them around the clock, but they're all delightful. Apart from, well, those that aren't.

When a **COMMON CUCKOO** lays its egg, it sneakily places it in the nest of a **COMMON REED WARBLER**. Because the cuckoo's egg looks so much like the warbler's, she doesn't realise it's not hers. After hatching, the chick follows its devious nature. Slowly but surely, it pushes the warbler eggs to the edge of the nest . . . and sends them all tumbling to the ground – crack! The adult warbler then raises the cuckoo chick as its own, feeding the insatiable youngster until it grows monstrously large in comparison to the elder bird . . .

Reed warbler

Common cuckoo

But let's not be too harsh on the cuckoo chick. After all, it didn't ask to be placed in another bird's nest. And it's not the only species that mooches off another family: *WHYDAHS* and even some ducks are 'brood parasites' too. It's a really smart way for parents to get someone else to look after their chicks!

So, don't be fooled by cute images of fluffy baby birds. No matter what we humans think of their looks, chicks can be bossy, nest-stealing, murderous creatures . . . and they're always hungry.

BIRDS AREN'T AT RISK

We see birds everywhere: on clifftops and car parks, above meadows and motorways. They can be spotted in almost any environment and even if we can't see them, we can usually hear them. Birds are just always there . . . so it might be difficult to believe that, today, they are in BIG trouble.

Birds have always had to work to avoid being eaten by predators, and to find food when it is scarce. But more and more are finding it tougher to survive. Today, one in every eight species of birds are threatened with extinction. And it's humans that are to blame . . .

There are lots of ways in which humans have made it harder for birds to survive. Turning forests into farmland is great for people, who eat the crops and animals that farmers produce, but it destroys the homes of the birds that live there, as well as the homes of the animals and plants that the birds eat. This deforestation is the reason why **YELLOWHAMMERS** are now 55 per cent rarer than they were in the UK in 1970, and why **WAGTAILS** across Europe are finding it harder to fill their beaks with delicious insects.

Some farmers also use chemicals like 'neonicotinoids' to kill insects that feed on their crops. These work well but can harm birds that eat crops that have been sprayed, by making it harder for the birds to orientate themselves while flying.

Humans are also releasing animals into environments that they have never in lived before, which is really bad news for birds. On the island of Guam, species such as the **WHITE-BROWED CRAKE** vanished after the brown tree snake was accidentally introduced to the forests by humans, and began eating the birds' eggs.

Brown tree snake

White-browed crake

Just as the introduction of pigs and rats killed the dodo hundreds of years ago (see page 32), the introduction of animals into new habitats is erasing many species of birds from our world.

Pollution is another big problem. Seabirds eat a huge amount of plastic, mistaking small fragments of everlasting carrier bags and toys for shiny fish, or accidentally swallowing tiny floating microplastics. As our planet's climate changes, bushfires are destroying the homes of birds in hot countries, while species from the poles, such as **EMPEROR PENGUINS**, struggle with shrinking sea ice that they depend on for breeding sites.

Emperor penguin

Although we will continue to see birds in our everyday lives, the number of species facing the danger of extinction continues to rise. But that's not to say that all birds are doomed . . .

WE CAN'T HELP BIRDS

Sure, birds are in a tricky spot. BUT that doesn't mean that humans aren't working to save them – or that YOU can't help!

You don't need to be a scientist to help birds – we can all support our feathery friends. In many parts of the world, including the islands of New Zealand, people are reforesting areas by planting hundreds of new trees, to bring native birds back to their ancient homes.

We can all help keep birds' habitats clean by trying to use fewer plastic objects and making sure we pick up our litter when we're out and about. If you're lucky enough to have a garden or a balcony, you could also try growing plants to attract tasty insects for your local birds to eat.

The more people know about birds, the more they can help them! Join a local birdwatching group to discover more about the species living around you, and write to the people who make laws in your country to ask them to set up protected areas so birds have safe places to live! Birds can't speak for themselves, so it's great when we can use our human voices to help them.

Experts are working very hard to protect endangered bird species. In Hawaii, birds like the *'I'IWI* (also called the scarlet honeycreeper) have been struggling to survive. Visiting humans accidentally introduced disease-carrying mosquitoes to the species' island homes, and the disease is fatal to the birds. Since 2024, humans have been working to stop the spread of the disease. By releasing special mosquitoes carrying a bacteria that stops new disease-carrying mosquito eggs from hatching, scientists hope that more birds will be saved.

The ultimate goal of a scientific programme is always to help a species thrive. In 2023, a small team of Brazilian, British and American scientists successfully raised two **BLUE-EYED GROUND DOVE** chicks by feeding them food similar to their mothers' 'milk'. If more chicks can be raised, this rare species can be saved from extinction!

So long as there are people who care and work together to protect the species they love, birds will have the help they need!

WE HAVE DISCOVERED ALL THE BIRDS WRONG!

With their hard-to-miss calls and eye-catching feathers, you might think birds are pretty easy to notice. After all, birdwatching would be a fairly pointless hobby if you couldn't, you know, spot the birds. But there are some bird species that have remained elusive, and some that are still unknown to science!

Sometimes, species of birds have been hiding right under ornithologists' noses. Lots of birds can look very, very similar, and scientists might only realise they're a different species when they take a close look at their DNA. This is how the beautiful *ALAGOAS BLACK-THROATED TROGON* was named in 2021, and the *CHAMÍ ANTPITTA* was named in 2020 (along with five other new species of almost identical songbirds).

Birds that only come out at night are trickier to spot. But that didn't stop local guides and ornithologists tracking down the elusive *PRINCIPE SCOPS-OWL* in 2016. Zoologists had heard the strange, catlike screeches of this owl on the African island since 1928, but only managed to study it well enough to describe it as a new species in 2022!

Satin berrypecker

Alagoas black-throated trogon

Principe scops-owl

Chamí antpitta

Looking in places not many humans visit is another way to find new species, although that species may not be new to the people who call those places home. The *SATIN BERRYPECKER* was first described by scientists exploring the rarely-visited tropical cloud forests of New Guinea in 2021. Who knows how many more surprising undiscovered bird species there are in the wild today?

Some species of birds have been known about by local populations or Indigenous communities long before ornithologists ever noticed them. Others have been deemed missing by scientists for decades or centuries, before being spotted and recorded again.

The **BLUE-EYED GROUND DOVE** hadn't been seen for 75 years until ornithologist Rafael Bessa heard, then saw, the beautiful bird he'd only ever known from photographs. Scientists think fewer than 20 of these rusty-coloured birds still live in the savannah and grasslands of Brazil.

The **BLUE-BEARDED HELMETCREST** wasn't seen from 1946 until 2015 in the peaks of the Santa Marta mountains in Colombia. Most amazingly, the fiery-winged, bright-beaked **BLACK-NAPED PHEASANT PIGEON** was filmed on a hidden camera in the forests of Papua New Guinea in 2022, an incredible 140 years after it had last been seen by western scientists.

With new species being named and others reappearing in the wild, it's an exciting time to study birds. But although it's incredible to 'rediscover' species that were thought to be extinct, it's sad that the species had become so rare to begin with. Unfortunately, the reasons why these birds became incredibly rare in the past are the same reasons why many birds aren't doing too well today . . .

NOW WE KNOW IT ALL

Congratulations, you've reached the end of this book! You've probably unlearned a lot about birds, and have maybe even been surprised once or twice. You've discovered how truly brilliant birds can be, so you might think you've learned all there is to know about them now!

Well . . . *not quite.*

Although they have been watched through binoculars, studied in zoos and kept as pets for thousands of years, humans still don't know EVERYTHING about the more-than-11,000 species of birds we share our planet with.

We still can't say when exactly birds became birds rather than feathered dinosaurs, and we're still not 100 per cent sure how all birds find their way while migrating.

We don't know just how intelligent lots of species are, and no one has ANY idea why **SATIN BOWERBIRDS** prefer decorating their bowers with blue plastic!

Most importantly, we still have to find out the best ways to ensure that BIRDS STAY SAFE. We need to ensure that they survive pollution, habitat change, hunting and all the other threats that face them in today's crowded world.

But the more people that love birds and tell their friends how some of the things they think they know about birds are WRONG, the better the future looks for birds! Not only will people care more about protecting the birds around us, they will also want to learn more about them – and that might mean we finally get answers to those tricky questions we still have!

So, borrow some binoculars, grab some friends, follow those chirps and tweets, and keep telling everyone just how amazing our feathered friends really are!

GLOSSARY

ANCESTOR A species of plant or animal that another, later animal or plant is related to.

BIOLOGIST A scientist that studies living things, such as plants, animals, birds and fungi.

CAMOUFLAGE The ability of some animals to escape being noticed by being coloured a similar way to their background.

CARNIVORE An animal that eats other animals.

COCHLEA A tube in a bird's inner ear, containing special hairs that react to sound vibrations.

CLIMATE The long-term pattern of weather in a particular area. Generally a place's climate stays very similar for a very long time – often millions of years.

CLIMATE CHANGE The variation in global weather patterns largely resulting from the increase of carbon dioxide in our atmosphere, caused by humankind's activities.

CONSERVATION The protection of endangered plants, animals and areas of land.

CONTINENT One of seven large sections of the Earth's land, including Asia, Africa, North America, South America, Antarctica, Europe and Australia.

DNA Deoxyribonucleic acid: a chemical code found in most cells of living things that contains instructions on how to control and build a body out of chemicals called proteins.

ECOSYSTEM The complicated flow of energy between animals, plants, fungi, bacteria and all other living and non-living things in a certain area, like a stream or field.

ENDANGERED Plants and animals that are at risk from dying out, often because of changes in their environment.

ENVIRONMENT The surrounding habitat in which an animal lives and must survive.

EVOLUTION The process by which a species' look, shape or behaviour changes from generation to generation, helping them to survive within their environment.

EVOLVE When the average behaviour or body of a species changes through time between generations.

EXTINCTION When the last animal or plant of a species dies.

FOSSIL The mineral remains of an animal that died millions of years ago. Fossils may be of the animal itself, its dung, its eggs, or an impression or trace it left.

HABITAT The living (e.g. plants) and non-living (e.g. streams, rocks) things that make up the area where an animal lives.

INDIGENOUS (ANIMALS AND PLANTS) Found in the place it originally evolved. For instance, the Bengal tiger is indigenous to India.

INDIGENOUS (PEOPLE) Humans that have lived in a place for as long as records have existed about that location.

INVERTEBRATE A creature without a backbone.

MAMMALS A group of animals with backbones that have fur, produce milk and generate their own heat.

MIGRATION The movement of animals from one habitat to another, usually to escape cold weather or to follow sources of food.

NECTAR A sweet liquid produced by many plants to lure pollinating insects that like to drink it.

OLFACTORY SYSTEM The parts of a bird's nose and brain that allow it to have a sense of smell.

ORGANISM A single living thing, such as a single bird, a single silver birch tree or a single bacteria.

ORNITHOLOGIST A scientist who studies birds and other closely related animals.

PARASITE An animal that feeds on another while it is still alive.

PECTORALIS MUSCLES The set of muscles that pulls a bird's wings downward.

PREDATOR An animal that hunts and eats other animals.

PREY Animals hunted and eaten by predators.

REPTILES A group of animals with backbones, which includes lizards, snakes, turtles, crocodiles and alligators. Birds are also now understood to be reptiles.

SPECIES A population of similar animals, plants or other living organisms that are more closely related to themselves than to other groups of living things.

SUPRACORACOIDEUS MUSCLES The set of muscles that pulls a bird's wings upwards.

ULTRAVIOLET LIGHT A type of electromagnetic radiation that is invisible to the human eye as it has shorter wavelengths than visible light.

VENOM Poisons that are injected into other animals through fangs or other sharp body parts.

ZOOLOGIST A scientist that studies animals alive today.

INDEX

A
Adjutant 28
Ali, Jarome 39
Anchiornis 6
Andalgalornis 6
Archaeopteryx 6–7
Argus 30
Arvind, Chiti 38
Audubon 29
Auk 42
Australornis 6

B
Beak 6, 7, 9, 11, 16, 20, 21, 23, 24, 28, 34, 47, 54, 59
Bee-eater 20
Bessa, Rafael 59
Bellbird 24, 25
Berruornis 6–7
Berrypicker 58
Bird-of-paradise 30
Bird of prey 8, 44, 48
Birdsong 23, 24–25, 27, 39
Birdwatcher 10, 36–37, 38–39, 57–58
Blackbird 10, 13
Bowerbird 31, 61
Brilliant 11
Budgerigar 50
Burgess, Murry 39
Butcherbird 20
Buzzard 8

C
Camouflage 23, 24, 28
Cardinal 52
Chamí antpitta 58
Chick 18, 25, 27, 30, 34, 43, 47, 52–53, 56, 57
Cleaning 9, 16–17, 50
Cockatiel 17
Condor 9
Conure 24
Cormorant 7, 15
Cowbird 25
Craig, Mya-Rose 38
Crake 55
Crow 45
Cuckoo 53
Currawong 27

D
Dander 17
Darwin, Charles 17
Defence 18–19
Dinosaur 6–7, 8, 9, 47, 61
DNA 32, 58
Dodo 32–33, 55
Dove 46, 56, 59
Duck 5, 20, 28, 52–53
Duhamel, Anaïs 39

E
Eagle 8–9, 15, 43
Endangered species 28–29, 39, 48, 54–55, 56–57
Eggs 18, 19, 33, 37, 42, 43, 52, 53, 55, 56
Egret 29
Evolution 6–7, 8–9, 11, 14–15, 25, 28, 32, 33, 39, 47
Extinction 9, 29, 32–33, 37, 49, 54–55, 56, 59
Eozygodactylus 7

F
Falcon 9, 44, 46, 49
Feathers 4, 5, 6, 7, 9, 15, 16, 17, 18, 19, 22, 24, 25, 28, 29, 30, 31, 34, 37, 41, 47, 52, 57–58, 61
Finch 20, 45
Flamingo 21
Flight 5, 7, 8, 14,–15, 17, 18, 30, 37, 50, 54
Flightless 6, 10, 15, 33
Fossil 7, 37, 39
Frogmouth 23, 28
Fulmar 18

G
Goodson-Fields, Indigo 39
Goshawk 27
Grebe 29
Gull 5, 34–35

H
Habitat 8, 29, 48, 55, 57, 61
Harrier 8
Hawk 6, 7, 9
Hearing 12, 13, 22, 26
Helmetcrest 59
Hemenway, Harriet 29
Heron 23, 29, 45, 52
Hesperornis 7
Hoatzin 20
Honeycreeper 56
Honeyeater 27
Honeyguide 48
Hornbill 28
Hornero 42
Hunt, Eloise 39
Hummingbird 23, 38, 43

I
Iberomesornis 7
Ibis 28
Ifrita 19
'I'iwi 56
Intelligence 27, 44–45, 53, 61

J
Jay 44

K
Kagu 15
Kestrel 9, 12
Kingfisher 16
Kiwi 12, 15
Kite 8
Kulindadromeus 6

L
Loon 24
Lorikeet 51
Lophorina 30
Luna, Álvaro 38
Lyall, Sorrel 39
Lyrebird 27, 29

M
Magpie 10
Malleefowl 43
Manakin 30
Mamalis, Louisa 39
Migration 5, 36, 61
Mimicry 26–27
Miner 24
Mite 16
Moa 6, 7
Monal 42
Myna 26, 51

INDEX

N
Neornithes 7
Nest 18, 19, 27, 31, 41, 42–43, 48, 52, 53
Nightingale 25
Nightjar 12, 23
Nuthatch 12

O
Ornithologist 27, 36–37, 38–39, 51, 58–59
Osprey 8
Ostrich 18
Owl 7, 13, 22–23, 52, 58

P
Parakeet 26, 50
Parasite 16–17, 20, 35, 53
Parrot 9, 23, 26, 29, 39, 46, 51
Penguin 40–41, 55
Pet 47, 48, 50–51, 61
Pharr, Lauren 38
Phillips, Eliza 6, 29
Phorusrhacids 6
Pigeon 5, 16, 32, 46–47, 49, 59
Pitohui 19
Pitta 52
Plover 19
Poison (and Venom) 19, 20, 21
Pollution 16, 38, 55, 61
Poorwill 23
Potoo 24
Predator 6, 8, 9, 11, 15, 17, 18–19, 22, 23, 27, 28, 33, 42, 45, 46, 48, 52, 54
Prey 5, 6, 8, 9, 12, 13, 21, 22, 24, 45, 48
Puffin 42

Q
Quail 17

R
Raptor 8–9, 12, 23
Raven 44, 45
Riflebird 30
Ringing 36
Robin 10, 13
Roller 21
RSPB 29

S
Sargent, Alyssa J. 38
Scansoriipteryx 6
Schalz, Sabrina 39
Scherrer, Josefa 39
Seabird 12, 18, 55
Secretary bird 9
Senses 5, 12–13
Seriema 9
Shama 51
Shearwater 12, 15
Shoebill 21
Sight 5, 9, 12, 22, 23, 37
Skua 18
Smell 12
Songbird 9, 51, 58
Sparrowhawk 8, 48
Spoonbill 21
Starling 26, 49
Sunbird 11, 21, 52
Swift 42

T
Takahē 32
Talons 6, 9
Tapaculo 42
Thornbill 27
Thrush 10
Trafficking 51
Trogon 58
Turkey 10, 46

V
Valencia, Lira 38
Velociraptor 8–9
Vulture 8–9, 11, 21, 25, 28

W
Wagtail 54
Wallace, Alfred Russel 47
Warbler 53
Ward, Jeffrey 38
Waterbird 7
Weaver 43
Wetherhill, Badger 39
White-bellied sholakili 38
Whydah 53
Williamson, Emily 29
Woodcreeper 44
Woodpecker 45

Y
Yellowhammer 54

ABOUT THE AUTHOR AND ILLUSTRATOR

DR. NICK CRUMPTON

Nick grew up in the UK on a diet of David Attenborough documentaries and hand-me-down Sega games before studying ecology at Leeds University and completing a PhD in Zoology at the University of Cambridge. He lives in London, England, works at the Natural History Museum, and occasionally teaches at University College London. His favorite animals are lowland streaked tenrecs, and he has an aversion to cobras (after one very nearly bit him on his bottom when he wasn't paying attention).

GAVIN SCOTT

Gavin grew up in the Dorset countryside where, as a young child, he would often be found covered in mud at the bottom of the garden, holding up a grass snake or some other interesting creature to draw. After studying Natural History Illustration in college, he went on to enter the world of character design and children's illustration. When he's not working, he enjoys rock pooling and fossil hunting with his children. He now lives in Somerset, England.